MAURITIUS
from the air

Endpapers: Those flying over Mauritius can see a display of waving green cane fields and stone pyramids, like isolated pawns on a huge chessboard. Here the sugar cane reigns supreme. Since it was introduced by the Dutch in 1639, who brought it from Java, all experiments have borne fruit in Mauritius. Today the sugar cane crop has taken on a mantle of aristocracy. Apart from its wealth, it offers a whole range of its silvery purple flowers at harvest time — a feast for the eyes.

Mauritius from the Air
Times Editions . Les Editions du Pacifique
422 Thomson Road, Singapore 1129.

© Copyright by **Times Editions**, 1986.
Second edition, 1987
Reprinted 1988
Typeset by Superskill, Singapore.
Colour separation by Columbia Offset, Singapore,
and Far East Offset, West Malaysia.
Printed by Tien Wah Press, Singapore.
All rights reserved for all countries.

ISBN: 9971-40-077-4

MAURITIUS
from the air

photography
ROSINE MAZIN
and
GERARD COULON

text
MARCELLE LAGESSE

translated by
BRIGITTE CHANG LEE

LES·EDITIONS·DU·PACIFIQUE

Contents

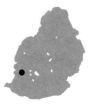

Many places have kept the name of the people who first owned them, and these people themselves carried the name of their lands in France. This concession belonged to Antoine Régis de Chazal de Chamarel. These fields, shaped like prehistoric animals, are a symphony of green. The horizontal and vertical lines of the furrows indicate new plantations and, between the deep-piled carpet of cane, the coffee plants raise their heads above Chamarel's landscape.

GREEN PATCHWORK

Those who look at a map of the island of Mauritius see a shape which looks much like any other. They don't stop to think about it, nor do they stop to carefully study its coat-of-arms which encapsulates its history. Nevertheless this island, which is almost invisible on a map of the world, was once a strategic point of great importance. Among a large number of navigators coming from several continents, it was known as a blessed haven, but the first person who let the world know of it was the Portuguese sailor, Domingo Fernandez. He landed the Santa Maria of Serra here around 1511 and, for several years, the island took on his name, according to the custom of the day. During the second half of the 16th century, the name of Domingo Fernandez disappeared from the navigational maps but reappeared for a last time in 1608.

Meanwhile, the Portuguese still retained an interest in the Indian Ocean. The name of Sirné or Cirné — the island of Cygne — had appeared on a Portuguese map and it was known as that when the Dutch landed in 1598. They renamed it Mauritius as a tribute to Maurice de Nassan, but settled on it only 40 years later.

The Dutch occupied Mauritius for a little more than a century, then totally abandoned it. On 20 September 1715, the captain of the vessel *Le Chasseur*, William Dufresne d'Arsel, took possession in the name of his King and named it the *Isle de France*. Yet it remained uninhabited. Six years later, it was given up to the East Indies Company. The secession to the King occurred in 1764. After the English conquest in 1810 the name of Mauritius, or the

Mauritius Island, was restored, without any decree ever being signed on the matter.

For the pilot who lands on the runway of Plaisance airport on a beautiful afternoon, the island offers a diverse panorama of greenery from east to west and from north to south: its sugar cane and tea plantations are coloured a tender green, the ripening of tobacco is velvety-green, then there is the raw green of English grass, pale green, jade green, dull blue-green; and a range of other beautiful shades of vegetation.

Nevertheless the contrast is great. In the middle of the fields stacked rocks stand as nature's unusual monuments — neither megalithic tombs nor prehistoric monuments from a former civilisation.

Among all this greenery and geographical grandeur, towns and villages spring up like children's drawings around a church steeple. The central range of mountains, which are strangely sculptured or covered in a variety of vegetation, plow deep ridges through the winding, mysterious valleys.

These valleys speak of silence, of peace at night, of a dog which barks on a threshold, of a horse which sometimes neighs at dusk when the faint glow of oil lamps or candles flicker behind closed windows. As these valleys empty towards the beaches, one forgets about the mountain and its mirages facing a new vista made for a legend or a drama for, over many centuries, the legends and dramas of this island all came from the sea.

In the pages of the history of Mauritius, once called the *Isle de France*, names of the most prestigious men in the French navy are carved in gold letters.

With the publication of this book it will

The White Tower, or Mount Thabor, is separated from Moka by the Plaines Wilhelms river, one of whose waterfalls beautifies the countryside. It was built by an English engineer, John Augustus Lloyd in about 1835, following the plans, so it is said, of Fort Belvedere in England. John Lloyd called it "Llewellyn". This name gave way to "The Castle" and eventually "The White Tower". Its last owner left it to the diocese of Port Louis to serve as a monastery. The Benedictine monks who moved in baptised it "Mount Thabor" and it is by this name that the estate is known today.
It is a meeting place for young Christians. Overleaf: A small boat, with its crew of fishermen, caught amidst the emerald green of the sea.

now be possible for the residents of Mauritius to see their "Island of the Sky" as though they were strolling on high with a lantern in hand. Seen from the air, what does it look like? Those adventurers of old who undoubtedly pursued great excitement in life, spring up like ghosts in every fold of the terrain. They were the men and women whose destinies were determined either by a guiding star or by a cross. Names from the past are colourfully brought to life and will make on retrace the roads filled with memories of yesteryear.

Ideas that took shape almost three centuries ago can instantly be pictured, such as the roofs of sugar refineries glittering in the sun, so far away from the first "*frangouriniers*" (sugar cane crushers), and the bays and forests, glowing and tantalising the reader with a thousand attractions and secrets of nature.

Time, History and Hope ... The Orient and the Occident can be found within this 1,152 sq. kilometers of land! On a latitude of 20 — more precisely between 19°-58' and 20°-32' south and between 57°-18' and 57°-49' east — this volcanic island, with its riches of iron, can be discovered, crisscrossed with streams which swell and overflow when the rain falls continuously for several days. A sky which at times loses itself behind amassed glowering clouds, condensed and ready to swirl, will soon be swept clear by a storm swelling on the horizon. Then when the sun appears again and the storm-ravaged fields are bathed in bright light, hope is reborn.

The rediscovery of all this marvellous scenery, the past and the seeds of the future can be experienced in this book.

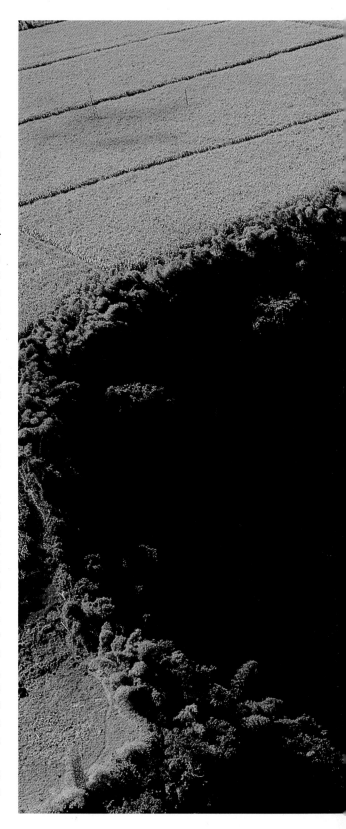

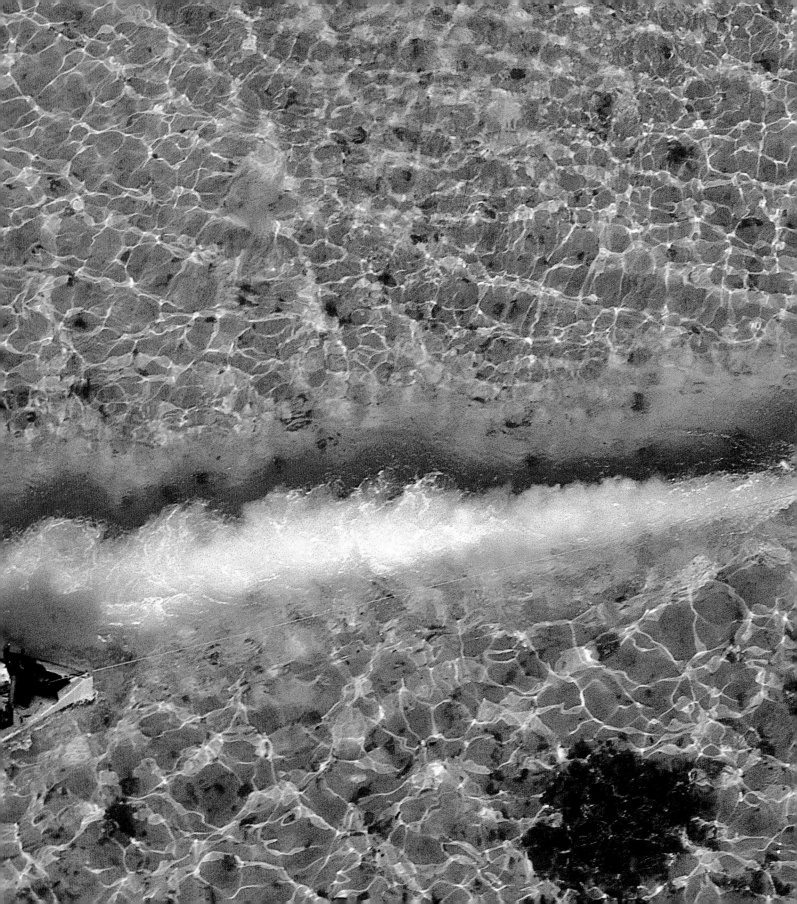

Among the last Creole houses, popularly called castles, is the estate of La Bourdonnais. It is still lived in by descendants of the man who built it in 1858. This photo shows the back of the house centred in its land, giving us a serene view to the south, right up to the mountains. Below the roof, a gallery which was once a lookout in the days when the full sails of ship were to be seen. On the left, a pavilion for guests passing through.

FROM ISLE DE FRANCE TO MAURITIUS ISLAND

The people of Mauritius are young, however, when they look back at their more than two centuries of history and more than two centuries of existence, it sometimes goes to their heads like wine. But what do they see?

The Dutch, lovers of authentic ebony wood, reluctantly went to Mauritius and left the first sugar cane, the stag of Java and the monkeys brought over by the Portuguese. But they destroyed all the dodo birds, decimated because they could not fly.

In April 1722, the first French arrived, having left for the Orient nine months earlier. The East Indies Company had informed the governor of Mascarin Island (Reunion Island) in the following terms: "The vessel *Athalante* departs in a convoy with the *Diane*.

On these two ships, destined for what they then called *Isle de France* (Mauritius), the Company has embarked 210 Swiss men, 20 women and 30 children, several officers, (an) engineer, clerks and labourers."

When they disembarked, no one doubted that many years of struggle lay ahead, that great courage, hope, and determination were needed.

To begin, to conquer, to dominate. These three words were impressed by Bertrand François Mahé de La Bourdonnais on the men. Meanwhile, the women were isolated, imprisoned in the harsh environment but seemed to be content in telling their men "Be calm, I am here." They were there, under the tent, in huts with roofs made of leaves, each to her own, talking of hope on an island where harsh reality ruled since only eleven out of the twenty women reached the *Isle de France*. Of the 210 soldiers, only about a third remained.

Three years later, following a census made on 13 October 1725 there were 20 officers or employees, 100 soldiers, 28 labourers, 5 servants, 13 children, 13 women, 24 blacks with the Company and 10 black private citizens, making it a total of 213 people.

The East Indies Company soon understood that the essential core of the society was not the individual but the family. Women from Brittany therefore arrived on the *Isle de France* to set up households. They were all married within a few weeks of their arrival.

As a little bit of everything is needed to make up the world, everything was needed to make up Mauritius. Cursed land, blessed land – maybe the first settlers couldn't tell the difference at times if it were monkeys leaping from one tree to another above them, or stags bounding from behind trees, disturbing the solitude; and they had to carefully put out the last glowing embers of a bivouac fire.

There were long months of solitude, agony, and deprivation, during which settlers searched the horizon for sight of a furled sail arriving from some faraway port by shading their eyes with their hands. A fluttering sail was filled with expectation, a sail briefly seen, momentarily lost and spotted again between the crests of turbulent waves. Men and women who came from elsewhere were full of mystery, with lips tightly shut on secrets which were for no one to know. Among them were families linked with one of the first families of the island. Royal officials, privateers, solicitors, officers and soldiers of the king's army,

In the south-west, the Morne Brabant keeps alive the memory of the Dutch who gave it the name of one of the Dutch provinces. It was a refuge for Black marauders. At the front of the picture, Ambulante Pass. During a violent cyclone in 1774, the Ambulante, the king's ship, left Port Louis with a regiment returning to France on board. She had no mast and no rudder. The ship drifted along the western coast and finally ran aground in this pass, which took her name.

humble craftsmen and labourers all came from every corner of France.

In the dwellings in the middle of the forest and in the town, children were born and died at an alarming rate. The parish registries are a record of hardship and tragedy. Among a dozen heirs, only one or two would survive. Time was short and at 14 years of age, girls already had to choose a spouse. Often more robust than the men, women married two, three and even four times. One of them had twenty-four children. Such a feat was not surprising on an island where to succeed was to show that one was more powerful than death itself.

Looking back at these people who preceded us in Mauritius brings up this question: from whom do we get the habit of this hand gesture, that curious way of tossing the head back and walking with hands clasped behind the back?

The 24 blacks with the Company, the 10 private citizens and the 179 French in the census of 1725 constituted the first two ethnic groups living together. Between the French and the slaves forcibly taken from Madagascar or Africa, an oral tradition was to grow up. The authorities and the church worked side by side. They fought against nature, against laziness, death, regret and discouragement and often against famine. It was already a melting pot, however, and there were lessons to perhaps be learnt from people uprooted from their Motherland.

All the beating of the tomtoms was born of nostalgia, and the *Isle de France* could not escape this bewitchment. Undoubtedly one night, when the first stars appeared, an elderly slave would have felt a strange resonance growing in him. A cry from the

soul .. a cry coming from the Motherland, springing from the forest to the hill, from the hill to the forest ...

Next to the fire the minstrel ignored him and the old slave voiced his complaints surrounded by a group who remained mute. The famous as well as the nonetities, hunted down by destiny, and all those suffering in exile sang along with him. It was an outlet, the open door on the infinite; it was the birth of *séga*, the local dance form stemming from the life and blood of the former homeland. The pain, the waiting, the release and always the oppressive climate. Quicker, always quicker!

In his own way, the writer is also an historian. He draws his inspiration from everyday events, sometimes as the humble observer and sometimes as the participant. He sees dancers glide past, curl up, flee and come back towards each other, torn and defeated ... he sees their dancing takes on a heightened tempo, agonizing in its intensity and filled with strange spirits ...

Life went on. Concessions were granted. Coffee trees arrived from Moka. An unusual machine – which we usually call the *"frangourinier"* (sugar cane crusher) — made of two cylinders which the slaves or animals turned, grinding the first sugar cane which was to become the most important crop for the country in the future. In the beginning there was only a sticky mass in containers shaped like a funnel and a rack. The refining of sugar was to come later, with the experience, accumulated from generation to generation.

Little by little the huts covered with palm leaves gave way to more respectable lodgings. At Port Louis, shops and a hospital were built as well as offices. The Governor's Mansion was built and continued to survive for centuries.

In this island, where everything was difficult, where man felt small and alone facing nature which was a threat to him, it was soon no longer just a question of conquest for those who came from afar. La Bourdonnais did not waste any time striking out at the ingratitude of the directors of the East Indies Company. After him one governor after another was constantly preoccupied with the defense of the island and the worries of feeding a periodically starving population, until the island was ceded to the King.

With Pierre Poivre, the *Isle de France* launched itself into spice research and, as a result, it established the wealth of Zanzibar.

It had a hand too in several long conflicts such as the war of succession in Austria, the Seven-Year War, the American War of Independence. To its detriment, it supplied two squadrons of men, ammunition and fresh supplies. When making ten thousand men pass through the *Isle de France* on an expedition to India, the Duke of Choiseul wrote to Quartermaster Poivre: "I am well aware that we will lack everything, but you are here, and we count on you."

An ideal port on the route to the Orient, the island slowly but surely became the star of, and the key to, the Indian Ocean.

In the name of France, navigators took possession of a string of islands spread out in the Indian Ocean: Rodrigues, the Seychelles, Azalega and the Chagos Islands... The wrecking of the Saint-Géran at Ambre Island laid the foundation for the fame of Bernardin de Saint-Pierre.

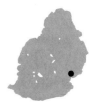

The Great South-East River acts as a border between Grand Port and Flacq. The bridge which links the two is far upstream. Near the estuary, there is a state-subsidised ferry to carry travellers from bank to bank. This is the island's longest river. Cane fields stretch right to the foot of the Mahébourg

Monsters of Apocalypse? It's simply the coloured earth of Chamarel. Still untouched by vegetation it remains an impressive and unique sight.

One is often tempted to ask what determines the greatness of a country and the answer invariably lies in the personalities of the leaders who were able by example and precept to inspire and motivate the men they lead. Nothing is more satisfying than learning about these people, and reliving the total love and dedication they had given towards the adopted country in which they were to leave their mark. For here are the men, sturdy as rocks, who shaped the past. One tries to understand the reasons which drove them to stand up to the seas. What good is it to search for logic? The magic of risk will never cease to fascinate humanity. Two centuries ago, oceans and faraway continents had held surprises for explorers. Today, it is the mystery of the skies which intrigues these explorers.

With the Bailiff of Suffren, great commander in India, *Isle de France* celebrated his victories upon his return by bestowing upon him an honor he would never forget.

Time passed, and life on the island continued. The populace evolved and had its *sans-culottes* (popular working class revolutionaries of the pre-industrial age), an exasperated group who were intent on taking over the colony. All of the royal coats-of-arms were removed. When the speakers got carried away to extremes they were called to order by their fellow countrymen. It was during this period of the Revolution that the *Isle de France* was abandoned to its own resources and had to tolerate a reputation for being a nest of pirates. From then on, its history is full of swashbuckling episodes of privateering, especially those involving Robert Surcouf and his brothers.

In Paris, Napoleon Bonaparte became the Emperor of the French. Shortly before being crowned, he named Charles Mathieu Isidore Decaen as governor of the colony. The situation had become so precarious that Decaen had to requisition ships used for trade to defend the island while waiting for help which had not yet arrived and which never came.

Yet, forgotten and almost neglected, the *Isle de France* gave the Emperor of the French people the only naval victory of the Empire; a victory inscribed on the Arc de Triomphe in the heart of Paris. The battle lasted three days in the Bay of Grand Port, after which the governor-general wrote to the naval minister:

"Your Grace, four English frigates, the Sirius, the Iphigenius, the Magician and the Nereide no longer belong to the British Royal Highness."

But it was victory without security. For the French, only their gallantry lasted.

Three months later, the British came back with a bigger force. On 29 November 1810, 70 vessels were gathered to the north of the island between Coin de Mire and land. At nightfall, 10,000 men marched towards Port Louis.

For three days Captain-General Decaen stubbornly staged a resistance against the invaders. In the morning of 2 December, refusing to risk his soldiers any longer in the sacrifice of an unequal battle, and assuming the responsibility for this decision alone, the governor proposed surrender. Weighing the clauses of the surrender one by one, Decaen wrote the last page of the French history of the *Isle de France*. Napoleon declared the terms the best ever drawn up.

On the British side, in a letter dated December 1810, from the "Camp facing Port Louis," General John Abercromby wrote to Lord Minto, the Governor-General of India: "I am pleased to announce that this island was given up to His Majesty The King by a surrender which was signed in the early morning hours.

The following day, nothing looks very much different in the colony except for the tricolored French flag which was replaced by the Union Jack, and they sentry uniforms which changed from the French blue to the British red. The victors took possession of the forts, batteries and vessels.

After the departure of Captain-General Decaen, on December 24, the first British governor, Robert Townsend Farquhar moved into the Governor's Mansion and on the 27th he held his first official reception. He also urged the residents to report to their village commander to support and sign the oath of allegiance.

If the residents of the *Isle de France* had hoped to regain French citizenship upon the signature of peace, the Treaty of Paris in 1814 drove home to them the futility of their hopes. As a result of this treaty, England returned Reunion Island to France but kept Mauritius.

After the takeover of the island, the law, bills and other acts were published in English and in French; however, the French versions were considered to be translations and had no legal power. It did not matter! French was, and still is, spoken while certain English customs were also adopted. Tea-drinking became fashionable, and the Champ de Mars was used as a racecourse ...

Photographs taken in 1859 by Herr Siebig, with boats in the sea-lane to Port Louis and a part of the town. They were "lithographed" by Messrs Hullmandel and Watson (Mauritius Commercial Bank Collection).

*"An echoing port where my soul can drink
In long drafts smells, sounds and colour;
Where the vessels gliding in gold and in silk
Open their vast arms to embrace the glory
Of a pure sky where quivers eternal heat."
Charles Baudelaire.*

In 1832, a move to abolish slavery without compensation was attempted with the arrival of John Jeremie, an agent of the Anti-Slavery Society, who was named Public Prosecutor of the Supreme Court. The Mauritians opposed this attempt by triggering a general strike. After the fourth day, the Legislative Council voted to dismiss Jeremie. The opposition, however, backed down when England agreed to pay compensation to the slave owners. It was a long and painful process before the slaves were able to win their freedom; some families were slaves for three to four generations.

This movement towards liberty was hastened when a fresh group of people came from India. Men, women and children disembarked one by one. New blood and new sweat poured into fields that were needed for ploughing. Already, mosques had their minarets towering above the island (although the Muslim immigration did not really begin until 1845), followed by temples in brightly shining colours rising between the green sugar cane. Women in multi-colored saris, and infanta eyes, danced tales of love and death. They danced for Brahma, for Vishnu and for Shiva.

These new arrivals brought with them their love for the land, this land of exile, and contributed largely to the opening up of the island.

In 1817 the total population was 87,847. It reached 183,506 in 1851, of which 77,996 were Indians. Of a total of 370,000 residents about ten years later, there were 117,416 Indians.

The Chinese arrived in Mauritius during the entire 19th century, at first in small groups under contract, then in greater numbers on a voluntary basis. Small businesses were set up and supported the economy of the country before reaching their scale of activity today. The Mauritian landscape was, therefore, enriched with pagodas of strange shapes, the *dragon* (dragon) and on certain festive evenings, the Chinese danced along the streets of the capital and young girls with wonderful costumes gracefully fluttered fans.

With the development of the sugar industry during the middle of the last century, there was also a remarkable boom in business. From 55,468 tons of sugar in 1840, the production topped 150,480 in 1862 and at the same time, a number of English companies were established at Port Louis. One could even picture for a moment, the reopening of the Mahébourg port. In the capital new quays were built and an incredible amount of activities enlivened the dry docks. In one year more than 700 ships entered the harbour. The reputation of Port Louis was at its peak.

Foreign visitors, each seeing the island differently, recorded their experiences. The collected works of these writers described vividly the way of life in the past.

After Bernardin de Saint-Pierre, Bory de Saint-Vincent, Abbot Raynal and Charles François Tombe, came Jacques Gérard Milbert who in his turn wrote:

"… I saw the harbour and the port filled with vessels from all nations loading very precious objects. The thrifty American, busy with his armaments, loaded objects specifically for the Marines. The British speculator approached him either to sell the cargo or to release it and continue on his route towards India or China. Those from

Left-hand page, top: Ecumenical Port Louis. In the foreground is the mosque with its minaret jutting out and from where the muezzin calls out his prayers daily. Nearby, the Saint Louis Catholic Cathedral stands on the square which bears its name. To the right is the Saint James Anglican Cathedral with its rising spire, built on an ancient gunpowder factory. Left-hand page, bottom: Port Louis, surrounded by its mountains, parched and yellowed under the withering sun. In the evening the sunset is a beautiful sight to watch.

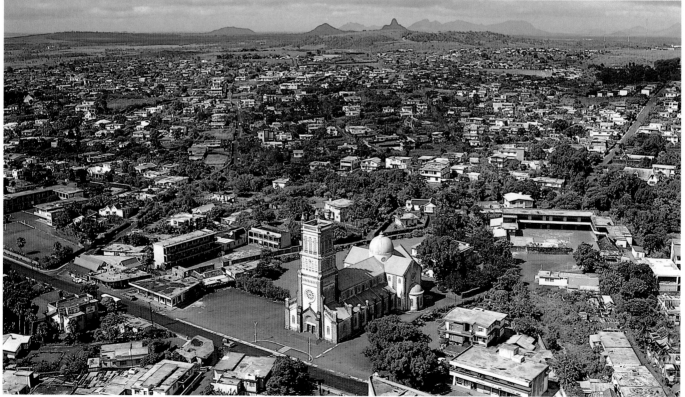

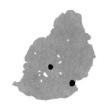

the Persian Gulf brought the rarest products of these beautiful lands; the Moor and the Arab from Muscat sold fruits and delicious almonds; the Dane, the Hamburgian, the Swede, and the Dutch coming from Europe or from Java, the Spaniard from Manila, those from Provence, the resident of the banks of the Garonne, the Malouin from Normandy, and a multitude of others came to anchor next to vessels of so many different nations whose flags unfurled on days of celebration, receiving admiring looks from their counterparts. This scene established a character of grandeur and wealth for the port which could not even compare with our wealthiest ports of France."

But what did these sailors see when their ship approached Port Louis at dawn? Most likely they would be greeted by the sun as it makes its way from behind the mountains. And the call of the *muezzin* (a man who calls Muslims to prayer five times daily from the top of the minaret), and the sound of the angelus from the cathedral tower, both echoing out to sea to welcome them.

And at daybreak, on this calm grey sea, which moved and changed its colour little by little under the sun, can be seen numerous masts carrying flags from all parts of the world, bobbing up and down with the drift of the tide.

Since it was restricted by a chain of mountains, the capital had expanded towards the north and south. Beautiful Creole houses were built along the streets and still charm the onlooker. Who cleared this land? Who waited, leaning against this balcony? Does one hear the chiming of a clock, children running, the soft grating of a harness ... it is simply poetry and a dream.

Beginning with mankind, one always comes back to mankind to forge ahead. That is perhaps why consuming material progress impoverishes us.

The character of the Mauritians is warm, open and born of an innate humour and natural intelligence; their zest for life can be seen everywhere on the island. The Mauritian loves his island. What does he know as he walks on the soil belonging to him? Strange echoes, perhaps the burning desire to hold in his hands a variety of grass scorched by the sun, or even this creek, with small boats anchored at dusk, giving the impression they were telling each other humorous stories and laughing, knocking together their hulls like ships.

The Mauritian is happy to share the wealth of his country with all those who have the opportunity to partake of it: like the splendid beaches, verdant fields and forests, unusual mountain views. In this island of breathtaking colour and beauty, hospitality is an old habit. It dates back to the early years, where a tradition of spontaneous friendship was developed among the new arrivals to the country. So if the new faces arrive now by air, they are welcomed with the same hospitality and warmth by the residents. Visitors who come to this island are often touched by this, so much so they may sometimes ask themselves why.

Well before the airplane, Mauritius had its railroad dispute, long forgotten today. It ended amicably in 1864, just before the malaria outbreak. This epidemic was the most devastating to sweep the island since the beginning of colonisation. It was the signal for an exodus towards the high

Left-hand page, top: From Ville Noire, the bridge which leads to Mahébourg crosses the La Chaux river. The town was established in 1805 by Governor-General Decaen, the last French governor, who named it Mahébourg as a tribute to Mahé de La Bourdonnais. It is in this bay that the battle of Grand Port took place. There is an old French house where the English commander Willoughby and the French commander Duperré were nursed in the same room. It now houses relics of the naval battle, furniture and objects which belonged to Mahé de La Bourdonnais, a collection of lithographs and other items of great historical interest. At the far end is the Montagne du Lion. Left-hand page, bottom: A general view of Curepipe, towards the north-east. In the background are the Piton du Milieu (Middle Peak) and the Verdun Hill. Furtherback, the Montagnes la Terre, Blanche and Fayence which, seen from this angle, seem linked to one another.

plateaus and the beginning of the decline of the capital. It became no longer lively at night, but only during the winter months when the shutters of wooden houses which had been abandoned during the heat were opened, when the governor and his family deserted the Réduit to move into the Governor's Mansion, when the horses competed on the Champ de Mars and when the entertainers from France gave rousing performances on the stage of the theatre.

The first steamboats linked England and India from 1852 with stopovers at the Cape of Good Hope and Mauritius, and sailing ships "tired of the ocean waves" gradually disappeared. But with the opening of the Suez Canal in 1869 which reduced the distance to Europe, Mauritius lost its position as an entrepôt.

Little by little the Mauritians realized their potential and their rights. They demanded reform of the government system as well as the legislative constitution of the colony, existing since 1831 and consisting of seven non-official members designated by the governor "among the leading landowners and tradesmen of the island." Most of these non-officials were British. However, the Legislative Council and the Government Council were nothing but advisors. The campaign for the reform of the constitution was supported by the governor, Sir John Pope Hennessy, and in 1885 it granted the Patent Letters which established a new Council, still presided over by the governor, with eight official members, nine appointed members of whom six were British civil servants, and ten other members elected by a limited electoral college. The introduction of the elective element gave birth to political parties and politics. From then on, politics filled the minds of the people, sometimes agitating them to action, but this was quickly suppressed. Another change was to take place in 1948.

Have the Mauritians lost part or all of their heritage? It must be patently apparent that they don't have one. The Orient and the Occident work together engraving with time a national and international history, amazingly shaped by traditional cultures, moral laws, a way of thinking often totally foreign from one to another. However, if the traditions are carried on, if the language is retained and if the memories don't die, what is it due to? Undoubtedly a profound mutual respect.

When war was declared in 1914 the Mauritians responded loyally.

When peace returned, a new era of prosperity opened with sugar prices rising gradually on the market. The United Kingdom became the principal buyer of this commodity. But soon there was global overproduction and prices fell. The revival did not last and as a result it discouraged single-crop farming.

In 1936 there was a real awakening of the proletariat and clashes increased as a result of laws which gave only a few guarantees to workers. This awakening of the working man preceded the declaration of the Second World War.

In 1939 the Mauritians were in British or French Free Forces uniforms. They could be seen on land, on the sea or in the air, in the lines of the Resistance in France and among the commandos who landed in Normandy. They knew how to die, like the others, with pride and without bitterness.

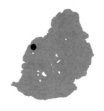

The lighthouse on the Pointe aux Caves (Caves Point) has guided navigators since 1910. This Point got its name from the largest cavern in the island as well as from many less important ones. Beyond the Baie de la Petite Rivière, the view opens out to Morne Brabant.

During this period, ships were sunk a few miles from the beaches and rationing became more and more severe. After abandoning a part of the sugar cane crops for food-producing plants, sugar production dropped to 138,000 tons at the end of the war. However, gradually during the next few years, production, which was 300,000 tons before 1939, surpassed 600,000 tons and stabilized to about 700,000 tons today. Tea became a secondary crop, but development remained the major post-war objective for the government of Mauritius.

With the coming of the airplane (a regular direct flight has since 1944 linked Mauritius to Diego Suarez and Johannesburg), the island became part of the international network and was to become the centre of the Indian Ocean.

A major change took place in the Constitution in 1948, with the right for women to vote and broadened property qualifications. Later, the provision of universal suffrage enabled Mauritius to move towards autonomy and independence. Since 1964 the Legislative Council became the Legislative Assembly and for the first time a chapter on the protection of fundamental rights was added to the Constitution.

On March 12, 1968 the Mauritians saluted their four-coloured flag and celebrated their independence. History repeats itself, for the student of Mauritian history will note that while progressing it also returned to the days when it controlled its own destiny under the Empire. In 1968, it was no longer a question of being assisted by privateers, but the breath of true liberty shook this island in the Indian Ocean.

The last English Governor-General was succeeded by a local. A Mauritian henceforth represented the Queen of England as the island remained part of the British Commonwealth after independence. The new constitution was similar to that of England with a prime minister and seventy members of parliament. Twenty-one districts were drawn up, each represented by three members of parliament except for Rodrigues which had two members. Added to these sixty-two elected members were eight "best losers" appointed to represent ethnic groups. Of these seventy members, nineteen including the prime minister, receive the portfolio of minister.

Nevertheless, the day after independence realities could not be ignored: the new nation's liabilities were a lack of natural resources, its distance, limited domestic and export markets, and little commercial experience other than in agriculture and sugar cane. To encourage diversification, in 1963 the government established certificates of development and in 1970, it introduced the certificate of export as well as Free Zones.

These Free Zones immediately attracted investors and changes were gradually made, not only for the country to open up new horizons but also to absorb a large number of unemployed, in spite of emigration to South Africa and Australia. Successes gained by investors are due to benefits such as a duty free status, free access to markets controlled by the European Economic Community, to which Mauritius is a member following the Lorné Convention, and non-taxable dividends for the first ten years of operations.

Mauritian labour easily adapted to modern techniques and played an important role

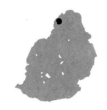

in the development of the country after independence. The number of employees in the Free Zone in 1970 was 640 and has spiralled to 55,000 today.

The cutting of precious stones — for Paris, London and Amsterdam — was the first industry to gain recognition for this island in 1986 and this industry now numbers over 277 companies, each holding a Free Zone manufacturing certificate.

As with the population of Mauritius, investors came from various continents — from France, England, India, Holland, Taiwan and Hong Kong. Among the products specially made for export (and which assure the island of substantial earnings in foreign currencies) are fishing boats, furniture, models of historic boats, shirts, T-shirts, gloves, dresses, blouses, toys and plastic products. Mauritius is the third largest exporters of sweaters in the world. Other products like vegetables, fruit and flowers — particularly andreanums (4 million per year) — also enjoy the benefits given to manufacturing companies.

A convention on preferential tariffs was recently signed with about fifteen African countries. Among the major importers of Mauritian products are the Comores, Tanzania, Seychelles, Madagascar and Kenya. Mauritius on the other hand imports meat from Zimbabwe, cement from Kenya, vegetable oil and textiles from Malawi, wood from the Central African Republic and other goods from various other countries.

These foreign transactions are facilitated by Port Louis which is fully equipped for the loading of sugar in bulk and the loading and unloading of containerised merchandise from its eight deep water quays. The airport of Plaisance, located in the south of the island, is linked almost daily with Europe, Asia, Africa and Australia. A bi-weekly non-stop *Air Mauritius* flight connects Mauritius to Paris in about ten hours. Works to improve the airport infrastructure are in progress and a new control tower recently started operating. As it now stands, however, the airport can only accommodate four Boeing 747's and three Boeing 707's.

Outside of the Free Zone, Mauritians invested in small businesses, many of which later expanded to include branches on neighbouring islands. Forming a more modest domain, small family-run industries require only a minimum of capital and they adapt themselves easily to the market and the environment. They often become satellites of larger organizations which buy their products. Banks and the private sectors contributed to the development of these small businesses by granting loans with low interest. However, much still needs to be done, even if only within the framework of technical training as initiative and goodwill are not enough to assure success. It is estimated that there are about 5,000 small firms employing 25,000 people, a substantial number in an island where 200,000 young are still in school and will be looking for employment in a few years.

It is also to be noted that the government is helping to revive Mauritian handicrafts, considered up until now as being of no great value, by opening a National Centre. Things have changed and techniques that were about to disappear are now being used, together with new ideas.

The population of Mauritius has reached

The Trou aux Biches Village Hotel, of which only the individual bungalows can be seen here, belongs to the Beachcomber group. It is situated on the north-west of the island and, apart from restaurants and shops, also has a busy casino. Some bungalows belong to the State and are used as residences for important guests and Heads of State.

one million and will substantially increase in a few years. Already 135,000 students attend primary schools and about 71,000 secondary schools where young Mauritians follow the trend towards computer sciences. Education is free in these institutions which are either State-run, belong to different religious orders or are private schools with teachers paid by the State. A French school, the Lycée La Bourdonnais, prepares the student for the baccalaureate whereas other educational establishments prepare their students for the Cambridge School leaving certificate, like the Mahatma Gandhi Institute established several years ago.

The University opened in 1965 and now has over 500 students. In the beginning it was forced to look into the immediate needs of the country and the University instituted reorientation and proficiency courses for many executives in the Civil Service and in the private sector. After twenty years, it is considering extending its programmes so that future students can choose from among the many professional courses it will offer.

It would be tedious to list the numerous organisations in which the sugar industry participates. The most important is undoubtedly the Institute of Sugar Research, established in 1953, and its goal is to promote technical efficiency and the progress of this industry in the area of scientific research. As a result, the country has been able to maintain its levels of sugar cane production despite the gradual reduction of land due to agricultural diversification, urbanisation and industrialisation.

The area for cane cultivation covers about 85,000 hectares, feeding 19 refineries for which the extraction capacity varies between 1,500 and 1,600 tons of sugar cane per day. The sugar season lasts four to six months and starts at the beginning of June. Sugar exports head for the European Economic Community, the United States and the free market. The Agricultural Chamber works in close contact with the Ministry of Agriculture and its major goal is to promote and safeguard the interests of agriculture. It serves as a link between the country's sugar industry and foreign institutions. The Sugar Syndicate handles the sale of all of its members' sugar and serves as an intermediary for payment.

Always concerned with progress, Mauritius has its place among the world's airline companies and *Air Mauritius* owns one Boeing 747, two Boeing 707's, two Twin Otters and a helicopter. As an island must have ties with the sea, Mauritian companies are owners of ships and its flag flutters on the oceans. *Mauritius, Belle Etoile, Beau Songe, Flamboyant, Tamarin, Jacaranda, Hibiscus, Savanne, Jamal Shah* and *Jeelan Shah*, these are names which are reminders of our shores, and they represent the tropical country in other parts of the world.

Since its creation, the Tourism Office has been playing a leading role in the tourist industry while coordinating promotional activities, overseas advertising and public relations. Small hotels of the past have given way to high class establishments capable of satisfying the most discriminating guests. Located on the most beautiful beaches of the island, these hotels greeted 150,000 tourists in 1985, coming mainly from France, Germany, Switzerland, South Africa and Reunion. Princesses and celebrities are among those who appreciate the gentle,

Looking like a windmill without blades (the dream of its builder), this tower in Poste Lafayette, a strange sight amidst the green, still does not spoil the beauty of the site. On the contrary, it makes you think of some solitary vagabond who has found, between sky, sea and land, a harbour of grace in a fairy-tale land. It is here, in the first months of French colonisation in 1722, that Second Lieutenant César Falliez was responsible for the first advance post, set up to defend the inhabitants against marauding bands hiding in the forests and mountains. Falliez Post became Poste Lafayette as the years passed.

calm lagoons and periodically return.

Deep-sea fishing attracts the die-hard, not only during competitions, but also in the off-season. Even then they dream of bringing back a chance catch.

Three or four times a year, tourists make stopovers at Port Louis for three or four days on luxurious ocean liners and they never fail to travel across the island in search of nostalgia. This isle has always stood on the route to adventure. Populated by a large flock of birds, it is recognised from afar whether from the sky or from the sea by its strangely shaped mountains.

The wind blows; in passing it touches people who came from all over — from Europe, Africa, Asia ... people who knew how to build the Mauritian nation. Together, they could tell the world with pride: "Look what we've done in two and a half centuries with a land without man, lost in the Indian Ocean. The courage and persistence of explorers made its history. The patience of their sons determined its destiny."

At Mahébourg, on the Ile aux Fouquets, the lighthouse, now not in use, once signalled danger to the sailing ships. It was opened in 1864, at a time when every ship that entered the sealane to load or offload cargo had to pay twopence a ton towards the upkeep of the island's lighthouses. Only those on Ile Plate and Caves Point still exist today.

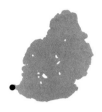

*The Morne Brabant looks
imposing and breathtaking
from certain angles. This
mass of basalt stands above
a narrow band of sand
which separates it from the
ocean. Located by the beach
are the Beachcomber hotels:
the Meridien Paradis and
the Meridien Brabant.*

THE SOUTH
The Coast of Legends

In the outermost confines of the Indian Ocean, the cardinal points on the island of Mauritius are of great importance. North, South, East and West — each point evokes images of sites which have almost nothing in common except for their beauty. To the east, the pastel colors of daybreak can rival the fiery sunset to the west. On either side, there are twelve hours of daylight. To the north, the calm sea and reefs are marked by a layer of foam as opposed to the south where the sea whips the coast and the cliffs with its storms. La Roche qui Pleure (The Rock which weeps), Le Souffleur (The Prompter) where the sea engulfs the rocks before retreating again forming drops of water like liquid pearls, La Tireuse de Cartes (The Soothsayer) sculpted of rock — all these are gifts of nature which are found only in the south of the island, in the town of Savanne.

North, South, East, West. The sea is forever, present.

O mer, toi que je sens frémir
A travers la nuit creuse
Comme le sein d'une amoureuse
Qui ne peut pas dormir

(The sea that I feel swelling
Deep into the night
Like the breast of a person in love
Who cannot sleep)

In the above refrain, the French poet Paul-Jean Toulet, who had lived in Mauritius for some years, sang of his nostalgia for the sea. He never fully recovered from the adventures of his youth — the lure of distant horizons, and particularly, Savanne at the height of its bloom.

From Savanne, one passes the district of Grand Port with its sugar refineries, and Mahébourg with its old streets built "as straight as a die". Mahébourg and Grand Port keep many memories of the past — in its museum, its cemeteries and its relics.

In the south, those who have a hand in tourism are very much concerned about offering the ideal beach that everyone dreams about — with its crowning blue sea, steep-sided deep-sea fishing boats, in short, everything that a perfect holiday on an island could offer. And on top of these attractions, a tour along the side of the Rivière Noire Mountain which leads to Chamarel village, known for the original color of its volcanic earth. Then past the Morne Brabant peninsula, whose name is derived from the first inhabitants who were Dutch, and past humble villages which dot the landscape between tumultuous streams and rivers: Ruisseau des Créoles, Rivière des Galets, Bain des Négresses, and Rivière des Amants, (Lover's River) which is modestly referred to today as Rivière Saint Amand.

Off the coast, the islands of Passe, Fouquets (with its lighthouse no longer in use) and Vacoas still control the entry into the bay. There, one can recall the resounding cry of Captain Pierre Bouvet on board the *Minerve* as he directed the frigate towards Passe and gave orders to his helmsman: "To the right." And long live the Emperor!" The commander of the division, the future Admiral Duperré was obligated to follow while being fired upon by the English rulers of Passe island and this incident was to culminate later in the grand and bloody victory of Grand Port.

Located on the west coast at Flic-en-Flac is the La Pirogue (Long Boat) Hotel, belonging to the Sun group. The hotel owes its name to the odd-looking roofs of the bungalows which look like upturned boats. The view stretches towards the mountains of the Black River, including the Rempart Mountain, in the background. Not far from Flic-en-Flac, at Albion, a diving expedition in 1980 discovered the wreckage of the 800-ton Banda, the ship of Pieter Both, Dutch governor of the East Indies, which was wrecked in March 1615. An important collection of Ming porcelain, which had laid intact at the bottom of the sea for more than 400 years was recovered. Among the canons was also found an astrolabe dated 1568.

The southern limit of the Black River bay. It was in the estuary of this river, on 9 May 1799,
that two French frigates, the Preneuse *and the* Brûle-Gueule, *were chased by five English*
vessels. In the distance, the Morne Brabant seems to rise from the sea.

Morne Brabant, in the south-west. It was once a place of refuge for slaves, but today it stands guard over two hotels, the Brabant and the Meridien, belonging to the Beachcomber chain. From this angle, one can clearly see the promontories which underline the way this cape resembles the hammer shark.

Tamarin, with its salt flats and its white houses by the sea, lies in the protective shadow of the Tourelle de Tamarin (548 metres).

Left: The salt ponds of the Black River and their silver reflections contrast with the surrounding green. It is from these salt marshes that the island gets its salt. In the tradition of the Ancients, bread and salt, offered at the threshold of the home, were the symbol of hospitality. The people of Mauritius, who often open their homes at mealtimes, have not forgotten it.

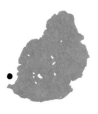

Ile aux Bénitiers, in Morne Bay, gives the impression of a lazy, languorous island. A very beautiful coconut plantation covers it completely. It can only be visited with permission from the owners.

The Meridien Hotel and holidaymakers who seem to enjoy the good life to the full.

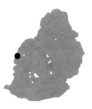

The bungalows of the Villa Caroline, with its red roofs among the tall trees. The nearby sea with its thousands of small curling waves encircle this magnificent peninsula with its stretch of fine sand.

The oddly-shaped fields of Chamarel.

Left: Chamarel offers the curious visitor at least eight perfectly visible colours, which sparkle in the sun. They go from chalky white to rust, passing through grey and blue. A geological curiosity, the remains of volcanoes, these bands are clearly separated, as one can see.

Le Grand Bassin, a sacred lake situated in the centre of the island, is the high place of prayer for the Mauritians of the Hindu faith. Each year in February or March, pilgrims come from all corners of the island and meet here at the lake to pray and take purifying water which they take back to the temples of Shiva. For three days, the long procession extends along the roads. On their return, all pilgrims — men, women and children — wear white. On their shoulders, they carry light bamboo frames called Kanwar, decorated with flowers, ribbons and even small mirrors which sparkle in the sun and on which they hang small containers of holy water.

*In the south of the island, Jacotet Bay recalls the first ensign of the Swiss Bugnot Company,
who came to Isle de France in 1722 with the first French group. Like César Falliez, ensign
Jacotet was commander of a post here. There is a small town on the edge of the beach.*

In the south of the island, the sea whips the coast with a torrent of foam. The now disused chimney of the old Savinia sugar plant can be seen.

Top: Chaland Hotel, situated between Vacoas Point and Blue Bay, near Plaisance airport, is much appreciated by the crews of the different airlines which serve the island. Bottom: From Corps de Garde Point, the view is directly across Blue Bay. At the far side of the bay, an English Governor had a bungalow built, which is still there. Left page: In the south-west, Deux Cocos island faces the Chaland Hotel from inside the lagoon.

From Ville Noire, (at front), the bridge which leads to Mahébourg crosses the La Chaux river. The island of Ile aux Aigrettes is located on the right inside the reefs.

A reservoir for the breeding of Macro brachium rosenbergii, *a kind of freshwater shrimp. The breeding follows a scientific method developed in Southeast Asia. The attempts at breeding have proved very successful in Mauritius.*

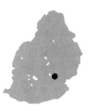

Riche-en-Eau castle has been classified as a historical monument, although it remains the property of the Rochecouste family, who also own the land. The Creole river circles the park before flowing into the Grand Port.

Port Louis: The harbour roundabout. Behind it, the statue of Mahé de la Bourdonnais, erected in 1859 by descendants of the colonisers, at the suggestion of English governor Sir James Macaulay Higginson. It was Sir James' successor, Sir William Stevenson, who chose the site, justifying it thus: "The statue of the city's founder will face out to sea, as if welcoming strangers." On the right of the Place d'Armes, the red-roofed buildings also date from the first years of French colonial rule. Once they were a bakery, providing bread and biscuits for the squadrons going to the Indies. Now they house the government printing press. In the background, at the foot of the mountains, the Champ de Mars, since 1812 converted into a race-track.

THE TOWNS
The Melting Pot of Mauritian Culture

Port Louis, Curepipe, Beau Bassin and Rose-Hill (the sister towns), Moka, Quatre Bornes and Vacoas-Phoenix (other twin towns) and Rose-Belle are the towns marked in bold letters on a map of Mauritius. Each town can recount a different history of its origin, although each complements the other and each is indispensable to the whole social and cultural life of the island.

In 1721 the name of the capital, Port Louis, was inscribed on a marine map drawn by Knight Jean Baptiste Yves Garnier du Fougeray. During the second takeover (the first one took place in 1715 in his presence), the knight was severely reprimanded by the minister for his zealousness. Nevertheless, Port Louis was established.

Since then, the central area has come to acquire an air of urbanity and civility, and depending on the hour and the day, it will take on a different appearance.

From 8.00 a.m. to 5.00 p.m. the capital is buzzing with activity, but thereafter it becomes peaceful and tranquil. The residents of the capital will peer out from half-opened gates or doors — which for a long time were used as carriage entrances — and look questioningly at the occasional pedestrian who happened to be along the criss-crossed streets of the town at dusk, for everything is closed: the offices, the City Hall, the central library as well as the library belonging to the Institute, art galleries, the museum ... .

At night the city turns its lights out with the exception of a few restaurants in Chinatown. There, if one listens carefully, one can hear the sound of dice being thrown and bets being placed inside a casino.

The other towns, by contrast, come alive when its residents return after a long sluggish day. Colleges are closed, but the libraries remain open. With the exception of Moka and Rose-Belle which do not have a town council but only a village council, all of the other towns have the facilities for accommodating lectures or cultural activities. Rose Hill has a theatre, a Salle des Fêtes (community hall), an art gallery, and meeting places where people gather to talk or to pay respect to a certain poet. Quatre Bornes and Vacoas-Phoenix have similar facilities and Curepipe is proud of its Carnegie library which is very popular among the students.

In all the towns, sports is of great interest and almost all these towns have their own stadiums. The finest and most outstanding complex is located in Moka where sportsmen of all disciplines are much encouraged by the superb facilities which spur them to aim for the gold, silver and bronze medals.

In Beau Bassin, which takes its very name from its magnificent lake, amateur and professional swimmers train at the Serge Alfred swimming pool which has a nice surrounding and where everything is taken care of to provide talented individuals the necessary endurance test and, where little by little, they gain confidence in a blue transparent pool under the sun.

A trim young girl emerges from the swimming pool, undoes her cap, removes it and shakes her head while her long hair becomes loose and cascades down her back where drops of water sliding down glisten in the midday sun. Not only is this poetry but it is the Mauritian youth marching towards the year 2000.

Rue Royale, a one-way street, which is not uncommon in Mauritius. Truckers drive alongside the handcart parked by the sidewalk. The shadows of pedestrians announce in advance the sunset, and the nights, when Port Louis takes on a sultry air.

Left: Port Louis, an unusual place where houses from days gone by rub shoulders with modern buildings. The streets are barely visible in this photo, and the trees, which one would not imagine are so numerous behind the fences, take their revenge, brave the heat and offer the citizens a welcome shade. A number of buildings, constructed of bricks and stones in the old section of Port Louis, dates back from the last century which houses the leading merchants of the capital.

Under the sun, along one of the deep water quays at Port Louis, multicoloured containers await to be loaded with products from the Free Zone before making their way to distant countries.

Right: Port Louis, seen from the sky and the sea. The Governor's Mansion, built by La Bourdonnais in 1736, still rises up, defying the centuries, among the groves of royal palms. Port Louis, where modern buildings tower over the older constructions, which nevertheless tell still of endurance and courage. Above them all, 10 storeys high, the Mauritius Commercial Bank building, decorated with a galleon, the symbol of trade. On the right, the warehouses of Blyth Brothers & Co, founded in 1830. On the left, the Customs buildings and in the distance, the deepwater docks. Port Louis has a population of 135,000.

Another view of Port Louis. Here one can see the vessels as they get ready to leave the port and hear the noise of chains as they are being passed through the hawsehole. At the entrance to the port (to the left) sugar is being loaded in bulk. The dry dock, Trou Fanfaron (to the right), retained the name of the first concessionaire of the site, Nicolas Huet, better known as Fanfaron, from Saint Malo, France. In the background is the winding two-way North Road.

Sir Maurice Rault stadium was inaugurated for the Second Indian Ocean Games in 1985. It is situated at Moka, and serves as a meeting-place for athletes in training and as a national competition centre.

The Serge Alfred swimming complex was built at Beau Bassin. This pool is named
after an instructor who was drowned while going to the aid of four young girls in trouble off
Pomponette, a beach in the south of the island. He managed to save two of them before being
carried away by a very strong current.

Overleaf: The Pailles region, near the side of Signal Mountain, has been one of the
principal areas of the Free Zone for the last few years. Textiles, clothes, shoes, electrical and
electronic products, plastics and other goods are stored here.

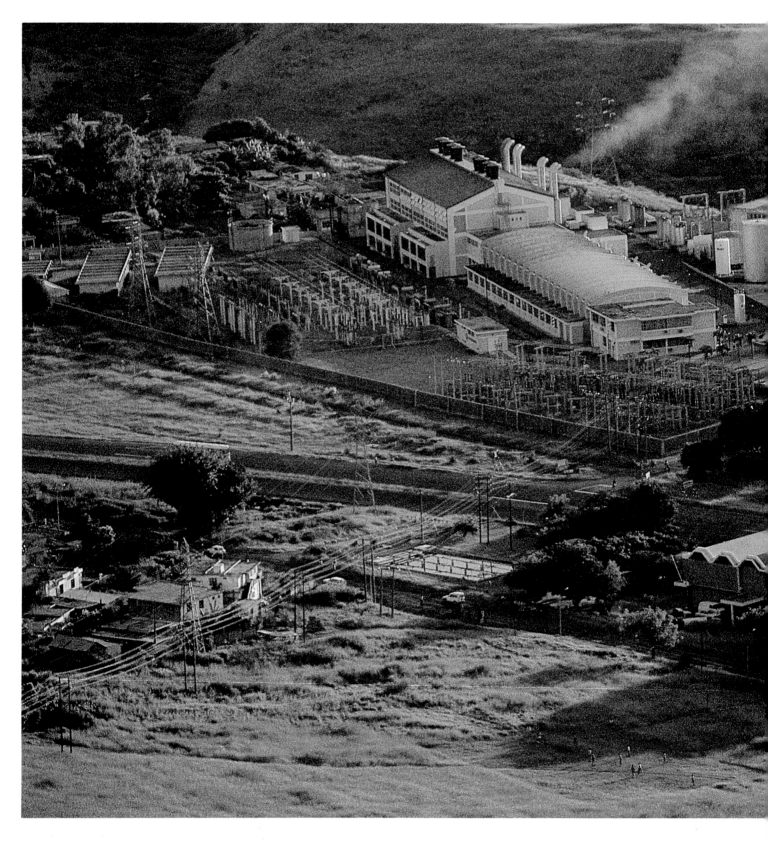

Réduit Castle is the residence of the Governor-General of Mauritius. In 1748 the French Governor Pierre Barthélemy David first built a small country house on this site that he had chosen. He called it "Le Réduit" and it was to serve as a retreat for wives and children in case the English tried to disembark. One can understand how this promontory, at the junction of two rivers, caught the attention of a man who, after God, was master of this land. One can also understand why, once he had built it, he wanted it to look different from all the other corners of the island. The years flew by, and after 1778 the country house became a castle whose design has since hardly changed.

Left: Tea was introduced to the Isle de France in 1770 by Pierre Poivre, a quartermaster. The method of planting tea differs, depending on how the crop is to be picked. If it is picked by hand, the tea is planted without symmetry but if it is harvested by machine, passage lanes are required. Aerial irrigation is commonly employed in these plantations.

*Four boundary stones
("bornes" in French)
carrying the initials M and
D (Mabille and Devaux)
once marked the two
concessions of Plaines
Wilhelms. From this the
present-day town took its
name: Quatre Bornes —
Four Boundary Stones. At
the entrance to the town, the
roundabout called "St
Jean" because of a nearby
church, is surrounded by
cane-fields and looks like a
magnificent, gigantic
French-style garden. A
miracle of aerial
photography.*

At the foot of a rocky spur
of Corps de Garde
mountain, a Tamil temple,
Shri Siva Soopramaniar
temple, clings to the side of
the cliff in the silence of
these wide open spaces.

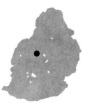

The Mauritians of Tamil origin dedicate Cavadees to the God Mourouga. This festival, which is the culmination of 10 days of strict fasting, is celebrated in January/February and April/May each year. The processions pass through the street to the temples from dawn.

The industrial city of Bambous, on the Black River road.

Right-hand page: Rose-Hill Town Hall (on the right). The main building houses a theatre, the Plaza, a room for shows or receptions (right wing), offices and a municipal meeting room (left wing). The other building on the left includes an art gallery, a library and offices. The theatre, which has recently been completely renovated, has welcomed lyrical and drama groups, members of the Comédie Française, Georges Thill, Jacques Brel and other stars including, recently, Juliette Gréco. Mauritian artists have also had great successes here, with operas, tragedies and sidewalk theatre. In the corridors, a museum brings to life again the great moments and emotions of Mauritian stars.

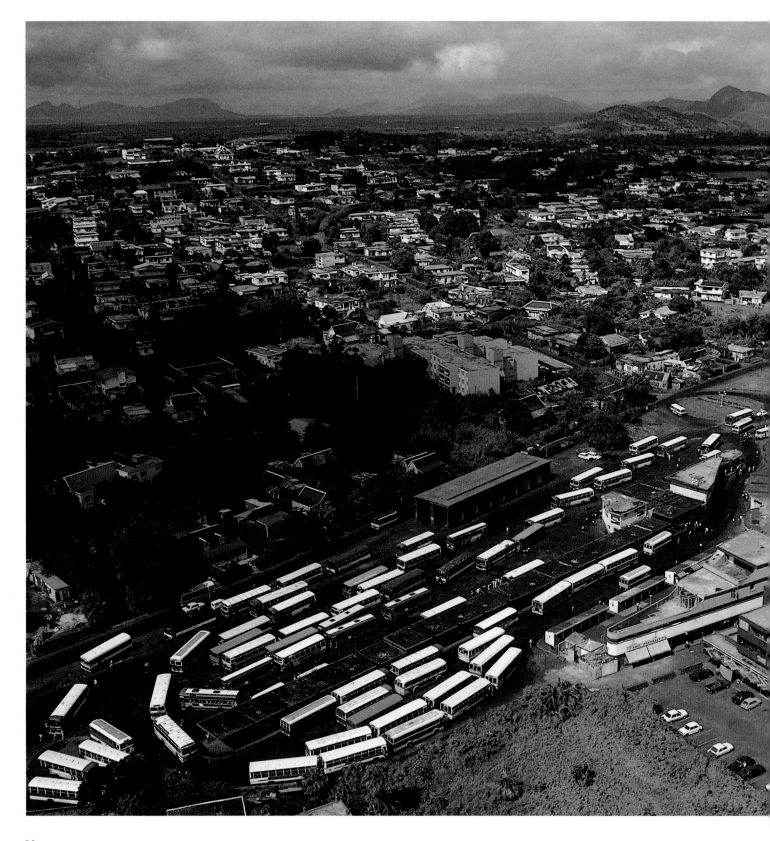

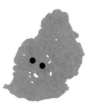

Weekly fair at Quatre Bornes. Market-gardeners bring their vegetables here and housewives hope to find some bargains. On the stalls, the red of the tomatoes called here "love apples". Piled on the ground, fabrics arouse the interest of passers-by.

Left: Jan Palach Square — the centre of activities of Curepipe — and its many buses. The market (to the right) with its lunar-like landscape is located in the centre of town where a few metres away, a gorgeous old house is used as the City Hall. Curepipe, a residential town 600 metres above sea-level has a population of 63,000. It was once just a stopover on the road to Mahébourg but the outbreak of the maleria epidemic in Port Louis during the middle of the last century had spurred the town residents to flee to the higher plateaus. The populations of the towns from Beau Bassin to Curepipe grew from year to year and the towns continued to spread out. The climate in Curepipe is very humid and the rainfall here reaches 339.9 cm a year.

The Basilica of St Helena
rises at the entrance to
Curepipe, on Curepipe
Road. It was completed in
1927, and was financed by
a parishioner, Mlle Hélène
Naz. The interior columns
and the balustrades are in
white marble. It is the
second parish church of
Curepipe. The first, in the
centre of town, is dedicated
to St. Theresa.

One of the colleges of Curepipe, Imperial College, at the end of classes.
Approximately 2000 students attend this establishment, on Victoria Boulevard.

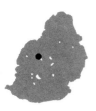

A view of Rose-Hill. In the centre, the spire of Montmartre church and the Convent of the Réparatrice Sisters; almost facing them, the Town Hall. The mountain is ever-present and worthy of its name, Corps de Garde — the Guardsmen. Although the recumbent figure itself cannot be seen well, the profile sculpted in the rock stands out perfectly. Beyond the mountain and the cane-fields, the sea.

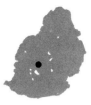

Le Trou aux Cerfs, an ancient crater, at the centre of Curepipe with a small lake in its depths. From the road which winds around the crater, there's a fine view of the town. At the front of the picture, the meteorological radar station, useful at cyclone time. The buildings begin to overwhelm the sides of the hill. From Trou aux Cerfs, on a clear day, one can see the mountains of Reunion.

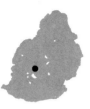

One of the very beautiful houses of Forest Side with a tea plantation behind it. In the distance, many opportunities to hunt deer, and the mountains of Mahébourg.

Right page: Villebague house dates from more than a century ago. It was built around 1860 on a terrace left over from the first French building. Mahé de La Bourdonnais and Athanese Ribretière de la Villebague joined forces on 21 July 1743 to found the island's first sugar mill on this spot. The second of these two gave the place its name. The property was then bought by M. René Magon, former Governor of the Isle de France and the Isles Sous-le-Vent. He died here on 4 October 1778. In the garden, the bronze deer overlooks the carefully-kept English lawn and flower trellises charm the eye.

Cap Malheureux village. The little red-roofed chapel, dedicated to Our Lady of Succour, has been entirely rebuilt with local wood. It is a landmark for fishermen. On Sundays, it reunites all the local people beneath its bell-tower. Whether in the magnificent bungalows or small houses, in the powerful ocean-going ships or fishing vessels, life goes on, simple or complex, as the climate dictates. It was near here, in Mapou Bay, that the English disembarked in 1810. Between Coin de Mire and the shore, some 70 vessels anchored and 10,000 men marched on the capital. Overleaf: The Ile aux Cerfs allows the Touessrock Hotel to offer a get-away-from-it-all break to its guests. You can take a day-trip there by boat, via a channel which borders the huge white sandy beach. Beyond, the ocean stretches into the distance.

THE NORTH
In the Shadow of the Filaos

Like a king overlooking his kingdom, the Pieter Both dominates the Montagne Longue chain. The North, a flatland, gently descends towards the sea and shores with evocative names or even names full of mystery. Why such a name as Cap Malheureux (Cape Unhappy) which lies beyond the sugar cane field plantations? Surely one does not recover a greater number of shipwrecks from here than from anywhere else? Why a Pointe Madras (Madras Point)? And who would know why a village at the foot of the Pieter Both, studded with streams and filled with sweet-smelling blossoming roses, came to be known as Crève-coeur (Heartbreak Village).

Emerging on the open sea are Ile Plate (Flat Island) with its lighthouse, Ile Ronde (Round Island) with its unique snakes, Ilot Gabriel (Gabriel Island) and the majestic Coin de Mire (Marksman's Place). On the slope of this rock and standing as tall as a cathedral, is a crack, a legacy of the past when each vessel of His Majesty the King of France shot a cannonball towards it whenever they were berthed there.

In the mid-18th century, Mr. d'Hauterive, a Parisian who had ties with the *Isle de France* and who was on a pilgrimage, wrote that Grand Baie would one day be to Mauritius what Trouville was to France. In effect, the north has become the mecca of tourism. The beaches are lined with deluxe hotels with their varying styles of architecture and visitors come in search of that which seems indispensable to their happiness. And in the shaded patches of greenery can be found filaos (casuarinas) with their rustling pine needles, standing next to a row of coconut trees. The scene is a refreshing change, an obtained haven.

In 1810, the British landed in the north, between the Coin de Mire and the coast. In the midst of what was still the forest and trees, they carved a road and marched towards the capital. This road is still called Chemin Vingt Pieds (Road of Twenty feet).

To the north-east on Amber Island the romanticist can recall the idyll of Paul and Virginie, (the young lovers in Bernardin de Saint-Pierre's romantic 18th century novel) and next to them stands Bernardin de Saint-Pierre himself, always on guard.

Private properties stretch out along the road encircling the coast and competes with one another in elegance and comfort. For the Mauritian, however, these properties are still referred to as 'Campment', as they used to be called since the olden days. Entire families then went in trains, cabriolets and wagons from the station to the beach during the holidays and camped in rustic lodges with thatched roofs and with walls made from the ravenala tree.

With time, everything has changed. Women who once shied away from the sun and covered their faces with a thick veil to preserve and keep their complexion beautiful have now been replaced by those who feel that the sun is never too harsh for them or their skin too tanned. At times they may briefly take refuge under cover of a small boat, lying on its side. Tourists have a choice of riding in one of these many boats found here with names like Alcyon, Taillevent, Alizé, Symphonie ... And perhaps he may choose the one on which the village painter had inscribed in his own unique handwriting in red letters: Saint Bole.

A daily sight around the island, when draw-net fishing is allowed. It is forbidden for much of the year. Here, fishermen at Flacq.

Left: Ile aux Roches, in the east, was first called Touessrock by the owner of the first hostelry, a well-known restaurant. Touessrock, which belongs to the Sun group, has since grown, encroaching more and more on the rocks. It has become one of the island's most luxurious hotels.

The rice plantations of Flacq bear witness to a long-held dream come true. In fact, as early as 1770, Pierre Poivre wanted to introduce the dry rice of Cochin China to the Isle de France. The results, it seems, were not good.

Saint-Géran Hotel stretches along a peninsula in the north-east of the island. Its name recalls the ship which broke up on Ambre Island's reefs during the night of 17 August 1744, a shipwreck which was immortalised by Bernardin de St-Pierre. The international class Saint-Géran belongs to the Sun group. Princesses and filmstars escape here to find the calm and rest denied them by busy city life. Everything is here — the rustle of the wind in the coconut palms, the murmur of distant reefs, and on windy days, the encircling surf of the lagoon. There are also fashionable boutiques and a casino. The swimming pool around the bar has its fans, but many people prefer the sea.

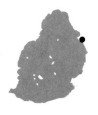

The peninsula of the Saint Géran has the shape of a horseshoe.

Notre Dame de la Salette, in Grand Baie. This was a parish church, alive with the devout and the supplicant. Now its bell-tower rises in the midst of the fields, alone. The couple who built it, M and Mme Louis Victor Mazery, and their daughter Adélia, have lain for more than a century under a stone in the choirstalls. The chimneys of disused sugar plants, crowned with green plumes, stand as a last vestige of the former human presence in the vicinity. They are not used now, victims of centralization.

Left: Beau Séjour Castle on the estate of the same name, is now annexed to Mon Loisir. It is situated in the middle of a park with flower beds, orchard and greenhouses. The grille fence isolates this haven and the gateway has above it the initials JL. Joseph Lagesse left the estate to his descendants, who still own it. In this sea of green, one cannot help but think of the grand occasions of yesteryear, the carriages, the impatient hooves of the horses in the early morning, the solemnity of the coachmen in livery. The crinoline gowns have disappeared and the parasols are closed, but the roof which sheltered many generations remains.

The sugar plantation of Mon Loisir, in the north of the island, wakes up to the first cold of the southern winter, in June. Around it, slowly but surely, the harvested fields lose their green covering and the sugar cane is sent on its way to the factories where the juice extracted from the pulped stalk is made into sugar.

LOISIR

101

At Poudre d'Or a monument reminds passersby of a shipwreck that took place off the coast on the night of 17 August 1744. In his account, the French writer Bernardin de Saint-Pierre reported that the name of this old town was derived from the colour of the sand, although he found it to be just as white as anywhere else.

Above: One of the lakes in the Pamplemousses Garden.
*Overleaf: Pamplemousses Garden was for a long time the King's Garden in the days when
battles were fought, not only on the sea, but also on the land, and for the land. From this
garden, millions of seeds and cuttings were sent to Europe, America, Oceania and the
Botanical Gardens in Paris. The most unusual vegetation arrived there. "The sailors bring us
things we do not know and leave us to guess where they came from and what they are for. I
plant them all the same," wrote one of the directors of the garden, Nicolas de Céré. The result
was that, in a few years, the garden in Paris was rated third in the world. Mahé de la
Bourdonnais, the Abbot of La Caille, Pierre and Françoise Poivre, Philibert Commerson,
bailiff of Suffren, Baudelaire and his Creole lady would walk up and down the paths …
And, who can say, maybe in the shade of these trees, a whole string of invisible people,
still walk back and forth.*

The pleasures of the beach and sea at the Trou aux Biches Village Hotel. Water-skiing, pedal-boating, sailing, excursions to the northern islands and diving — these are some of the choices available. Or you can visit Mon Choisy Bay (at the upper end), Pointe aux Canonniers where Club Méditerranée is located, or even Coin de Mire which "resembles a fortress in the midst of the waves" according to the French writer Bernardin de Saint-Pierre.

Left: The rugged-looking Royal Palm Hotel blends in nicely with its surroundings.

At front of picture, the Grand Baie Club, a private club which, several times a year, is the starting point of a sailboard regatta around the island. It attracts the foremost sailboarders of the Indian Ocean region and even Europe. On its right, in the centre of the photograph, the Royal Palm, a luxurious Beachcomber hotel, attracts numerous stars of stage and screen, who come here to unwind in comfort and luxury.

This small peninsula marks the boundary of the Grand Baie region.

It was at Pointe aux Canonniers that Club Mediterranée chose to build its bungalows in 1974. Since then, the number of tourists has continued to grow, so much so that new buildings have been erected. From this promontory, the view takes in Coin de Mire, advance sentinel to the north.

*Grand Gaube ("gaube"
once meant "small bay") in
the north-east of the island.
The chapel is under the
patronage of St Michael,
and a pilgrimage is held
here each year on 29
September. In the shade of
the great trees, the marine
carpenters build and finish
the vessles used for fishing
on the open sea.*

A Tamil temple at Grand Baie.

Left: Hindu temple complex at Triolet. The faithful come here in large numbers for religious ceremonies. The foreigner who comes should have the rites explained to him if he wants to fully understand the spiritual aspects in their original simplicity.

The P.L.M. hotel of the Pullman group, which was recently built at Trou aux Biches, offers guests an architecture where charm depends essentially on how it is perceived. Verandas stretch out towards the open sea providing the guests with welcome shade while they cool themselves and relax.

Right: Further to the north, on the same longitude as Coin de Mire, the Merville Hotel offers its clients a harmonious setting on a site where the softness of the sand makes the jade green sea seem almost aggressive.

These islands are scattered to the north of Mauritius. Coin de Mire, an outpost off Cap Malheurex "resembles a fortress in the midst of the waves", as Bernardin de St-Pierre described it. After dusk, Ile Plate, friend of seamen, sends a ray of light from its lighthouse across the sea. Ile Plate is joined to a small island, Ilot Gabriel, by reefs which can clearly be seen at low tide. In the distance, Ile Ronde, (which is not really round) with its native palm trees, its harmless snakes and its great lizard, unique in the world. On the other hand, Ile aux Serpents (Snake Island) has no snakes and is round. Who started this confusion?

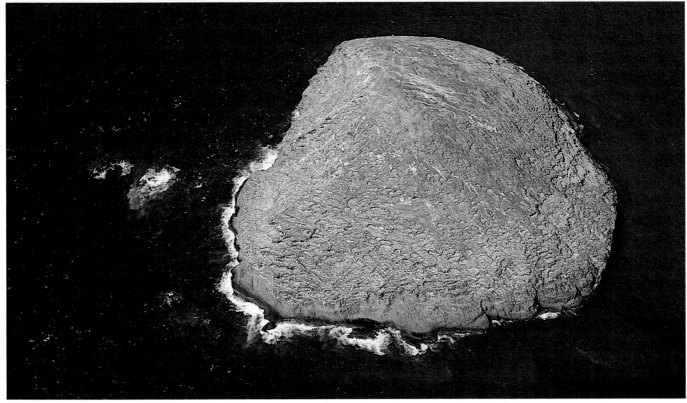

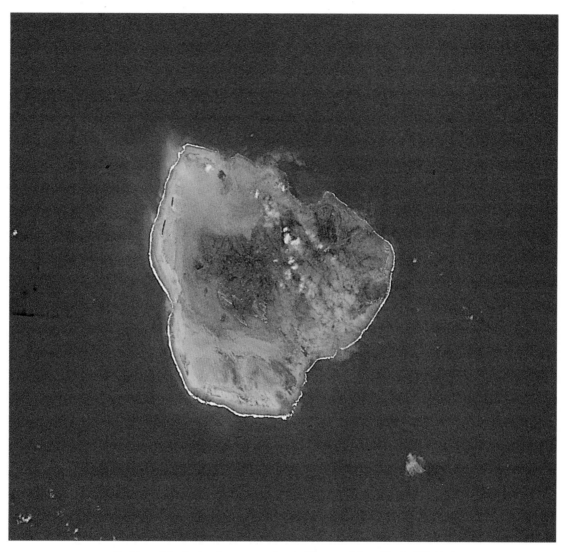

Rodrigues Island taken from a space shuttle. Photograph issued by the US National Aeronautics and Space Administration (NASA).

RODRIGUES

The island of Rodrigues was discovered around 1534–1536 by the Portuguese seaman, Diego Rodriguez, who named it after himself. It still retains his name today. The island is located 63°20'-63°30' east and 19°40'-19°46' south, at about 353 nautical miles east of Mauritius. Of volcanic origin, it has a land area of 42 square miles. Its population stands at around 35,000, originating from Mauritius.

France took possession of this island in 1726, without immediately establishing a settlement, and with the other Indian Ocean islands it became a dependency of Mauritius, then known as the *Isle de France*.

With independence given to Mauritius in 1968, Rodrigues became an integral part of its territory and formed the twenty-first district of Mauritius with two members of parliament, elected by universal suffrage, representing the island in the Mauritian Parliament.

Rodrigues is administered by a civil servant with the title of Administrative Secretary and justice is handled by a Mauritian judge who visits the island at regular intervals.

Rodrigues is served by sea, by the *S.S. Mauritius*, about fifteen times a year. In 1972, a landing strip was built at Pointe Coral and an *Air Mauritius* Twin Otter now links the two islands four times a week — or more often if necessary.

The main port is Port Mathurin in the north; the other port, Port Sud-Est, is only accessible to boats with a shallow draught, and even then only when absolutely necessary since the difficult approach demands a masterly knowledge of the area.

The hills of Rodrigues are rugged and its reefs extend far out into the sea. There are numerous bays and coves on the coast and capes on peaks have evocative names such as Malgache Bay, Pistache Bay, Manioc Bay, Tamarin Cove, Ally Cove ... Peaks are named: Cotton Peak, Venus Peak (Venus was spotted in 1761), Devil Peak, Pursuit Peak, La Gueule Peak ... Small volcanic or coral islands surround the main island, sitting in their own reflections.

Long neglected, Rodrigues only had its first road built in 1880 after a visit by an English governor, and only at the beginning of the twentieth century was it linked to Mauritius by cables of the *Eastern Telegraph Company*. Today there are 125 direct telephone lines with Mauritius. For the last 75 years, steamboats have replaced sailing craft, a change that brings with it manifold advantages.

The main services are controlled by Mauritian civil servants; they can be found in hospitals, police, social security, prisons and many other postings. These civil servants live at Port Mathurin whereas the residents of Rodrigues choose to live in the interior or coastal regions of the island.

As in Mauritius, education is free. There are ten primary schools, of which five are State-run and five Catholic, two secondary schools, and the Rodrigues College, a State school located in Maréchal which admits children from Rodrigues. However, secondary school classes do not go beyond Form IV and those who want to sit for the Cambridge certificate have to complete their education in Mauritius.

The cooperative movement is active and

Cotton Point, in the east, one of the island's most beautiful spots. In 1809, Lieutenant-Colonel Henry Keating found, in Rodrigues, a cotton plant which seemed to him to be superior in quality to that grown in India. Several sailing boats have been shipwrecked on the coast off Rodrigues, particularly in the east.

Left: Port Mathurin, the capital of Rodrigues. The plan of the town was laid in 1864 by James William Duncan, a surveyor. The photo shows the straight lines of the streets. Work on the port some years ago has given ships access to a new dock. On the hills, inhabited areas can be seen. When the supply ship is in, the inhabitants take the opportunity to come to the town with their livestock for export.

it pools together associations for the production of onions and garlic and those of the Producers and Farmers. Livestock breeders export beef, mutton, baby goats, pork and poultry to Mauritius. On the other hand, the sale of onions is made by the Marketing Board of Mauritius. Fishermen's cooperatives, with one woman representative, grouped themselves into a federation. The Fishermen's Centre, with a freezer room, was built and two youngsters from Rodrigues are now sharing their knowledge with their colleagues after receiving a two-year training course in Mauritius.

Tourism is not forgotten. There is one hotel at Pointe Venus and *pensions* greet guests with a warm welcome. The visitor can take nature or fishing excursions, search for legendary treasure or visit caves in the wild hope of discovering a Solitaire skeleton — a bird described by François Leguat, a French Huguenot who, with seven companions, attempted to set up the first French firm in Rodrigues that welcome French Protestant exiles. From this trip (1691–1693), Leguat was to record a particularly interesting account of the island's flora and fauna.

At the time that Isle de France was conquered by the British, Rodrigues served as a rendezvous point for fleets coming from India and the Cape of Good Hope. There were many shipwrecks on the reefs of this island which had no lighthouses to warn them.

Rodrigues. Island of memories. Seen from the air, will Rodrigues reveal secrets it has so jealously guarded until now? For the first time, it is allowing a rendezvous without compare.

Pâté Reynieux, not far from South-East Port, is a giant black stain on the turquoise blue of the sea, not far from the Pointe des Courants (Sea Currents) and the Enfoncement des Chauves-Souris.

INDEX

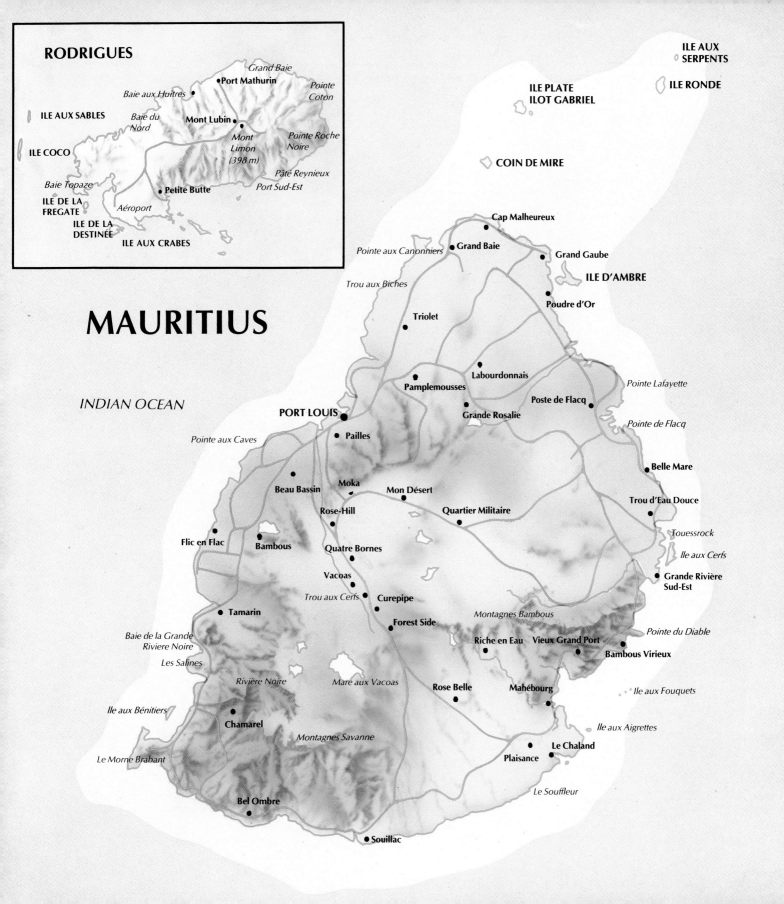

RODRIGUES

Grand Baie
● Port Mathurin
Baie aux Huîtres
Pointe Coton
ILE AUX SABLES
Baie du Nord
● **Mont Lubin**
ILE COCO
Mont Limon (398 m)
Pointe Roche Noire
Baie Topaze
Pâté Reynieux
ILE DE LA FREGATE
Aéroport
● **Petite Butte**
Port Sud-Est
ILE DE LA DESTINÉE
ILE AUX CRABES

MAURITIUS

ILE AUX SERPENTS

ILE PLATE ILOT GABRIEL

ILE RONDE

◇ **COIN DE MIRE**

Cap Malheureux ●
Pointe aux Canonniers
● **Grand Baie**
Grand Gaube ●
Trou aux Biches
ILE D'AMBRE
Poudre d'Or ●
● Triolet
Labourdonnais ●
Pointe Lafayette
● **Pamplemousses**
Poste de Flacq ●
Grande Rosalie ●
Pointe de Flacq
INDIAN OCEAN
PORT LOUIS ●
Pointe aux Caves
● Pailles
● **Belle Mare**
● Moka
Mon Désert ●
Beau Bassin ●
Trou d'Eau Douce ●
● Rose-Hill
Quartier Militaire ●
Touessrock
Flic en Flac ●
Ile aux Cerfs
Bambous ●
Quatre Bornes ●
Vacoas ●
Grande Rivière Sud-Est ●
Trou aux Cerfs
Curepipe ●
Forest Side ●
Montagnes Bambous
● **Tamarin**
Pointe du Diable
Baie de la Grande Rivière Noire
Riche en Eau ●
Vieux Grand Port ●
Bambous Virieux
Les Salines
Rivière Noire
Maré aux Vacoas
Mahébourg ●
Ile aux Fouquets
Ile aux Bénitiers
Rose Belle ●
● **Chamarel**
Montagnes Savanne
Ile aux Aigrettes
● **Le Chaland**
Plaisance ●
Le Morne Brabant
Le Souffleur
● **Bel Ombre**
● **Souillac**

ACKNOWLEDGEMENTS

The authors and the publisher would like to
thank for their help Mrs Banymandhub,
Mr. Bhoyrul and Mr. Chidambaram of Air
Mauritius, and Mrs Bhuckory of the
Mauritius Government Tourist Office.

Translation of the captions by Dr June Kane
and Brigitte Chang Lee.

Photo credits: All photographs in this book are
by Rozine Mazin with the exception of
pages 10-11, 22 (top), 59, 81 (right), 83, 88,
104-105, 106 which are by Gérard Coulon.

Printed in Singapore
March 1988